The 80/20 STRATEGY:

A Simple Approach for Getting A's on All Quizzes, Tests, and Exams

By

Dr. David Addie Noye

Ebook formatting by www.ebooklaunch.com

An e-book edition of this title is available on www.smashwords.com and www.the8020strategy.com

PREFACE

The purpose of this book is to help students to reduce test or exam preparation and taking anxieties by guiding learners to use a **syllabus** as a **roadmap** for **achieving HIGH scores** on **all quizzes, tests and exams**. This book recognizes that many students are not able to do well on quizzes, tests and exams because they employ inefficient methods and/or lack simple strategies. Although several books have been written to aid students on the subject matter, they seem not to adequately address the needs of students, thus many students struggle and unsuccessfully search for other substitutes. It has also been noticed that lack of appropriate comprehensive tests and exams passing guides eventually result in poor class grades, poor GPAs and in some instances students drop out of school or college. In addition to other test or exam taking aids that students may be privy to, this book is designed to focus on providing an overriding quiz, test and exam preparation, revision as well taking strategies: The 80/20 Strategy.

The 80-20 Strategy is, therefore, a simple approach made of a three-phase tests and exams passing system consisting of the methods for (a) preparing for tests, (b) revising for tests, and (c) taking exams. This book also serves as a roadmap and encourages and guide learners to complete all course requirements from the beginning of any training or teaching program to enjoy learning, achieve high scores, and gain greater academic success. In this book, the words exam and test are sometimes used interchangeably. However, test is used to cover all course requirements such as attendance, quizzes, assignments, experiments, projects, midterm exams and final exams, and on the other hand, exam is used specifically for tests such as midterm, final exams, standardized tests and certification exams.

To provide an overview for students, this book, answers these questions: (a) when, how and what to do to start preparing for tests or exams, (b) when and what system is efficient for revising for an exam or a test, and (c) what are the plans including psychological techniques for taking an exam or a test. The tips or instructions or guidelines, given in this book apply to tests and examinations in general.

Particularly, this book will benefit the college and university students, and provide a roadmap on what to do at the start of the semester through to the end of the semester to excel on all the course requirements in order to achieve higher scores on all class tests as well as higher overall GPAs. It will also benefit high school students. Additionally, the book can be of help to people who are taking online courses and other professional exams to either advance or change or upgrade their careers. It may also be of use to some teachers, instructors, and professors who are looking for alternative ways to motivate some specific students that need help in other ways. This guide prescribes 80/20 strategy, which is a proven three-phase test and exam passing system to apply to get highest scores, "A" grades and highest GPAs in any academic, instructional, training and educational program.

TABLE OF CONTENTS

1.0 INTRODUCTON

1.1 Why This Book?

From childhood, I always forgot everything I was asked to do but I am able to achieve all my academic feats including a GPA of 3.82 at the doctorate level. Till today, when I put food in the cooker I will forget, and in the next minute, the food will burn. I remember when I was in elementary school, one of my senior brothers always complained to me, "You always forget everything you are asked to do, but how do you pass your exams in school?" Being a forgetful person, I am now ready to share the technique, I have named the 80/20 Strategy that I have developed and successfully practiced over the years and used to pass all my tests including standard and final exams through my Bachelors, Masters and Doctorate education and in the process studying and passing tough courses including nanotechnology.

In 1989, I made notes based on my examination passing techniques to publish a book, but I was not able to do that because I became busy with other exciting projects. However, over the years, families and friends at college and university have asked me, "Prof, how do I study to pass my examinations?" I will then take my old notes on how to prepare and pass exams successfully and share with them.

All these friends who used the test passing techniques, passed their exams successfully, graduated from college and are all happy with their lives. Remember, I am a scientist and engineer, but in 2010, a friend who is Law Professor, called Ms. Dzidzo Amoa asked me to make a presentation to her law students on how to study and pass exams. I took my old notes and presented to the law students, and it was well received. In the law school, the students may have bachelor's and master's degrees and in some cases doctorate degrees pursuing the law degree. Notwithstanding, all these accomplished students still need little guidance or tips to go through their education. After that presentation, I continued to share my examination passing techniques with friends and families. This current book is in part based on that performance.

However, on February 20, 2017, after listening to a webinar by Eben Pagan on how to make digital products that sell themselves, I thought it is now time to make the over 33 years of examination preparation and passing techniques available to the general public, especially to college students. This passing exam technique works for all kinds of examinations and tests including professional examinations irrespective of the field. More importantly, this current book as structured will benefit college and university students to achieve and maintain excellent scores, grades, and GPAs. In fact, this book could also be beneficial to high school students and people who are taking professional or certification exams to upgrade their careers. Instructors, teachers, and professors may also find the book helpful, especially, if the intent is to help specific student(s) struggling in class who need alternative study guide and exam passing techniques.

1.2 Organization of The Book

Tests in the context of this book are course evaluation criteria commonly used to assess students for a course. These include class assignments, homework assignments, quizzes, experiments, projects, and examinations. This book focuses on (a) methods and systems for preparing for these tests from the beginning of the semester, (b) system and practices for revising to take tests and exams, and (c) exam-taking or test-taking techniques. The book focuses directly on providing hints and ideas on how to score high on all given tests and to achieve and maintain excellent grades and GPAs at end of any learning or instructional or training or educational program including a semester program for colleges and universities.

This introduction section highlights why the author wrote this book based on his background experiences of test preparation and exam taking techniques proven for over 33 years which reflects on the author's academic accomplishments. To quickly follow this guide, it is broken into three main parts: Part 1 - Preparing for the Tests and Exams, Part 2 - Revising for the Tests and Exams, and Part 3 - Taking the Tests and Exams.

Part 1: Preparing for the tests and exams covers physical and psychological preparation right from the beginning of the semester. To pass all tests and get excellent scores and GPAs do not begin at the revision or the day of the exams, it starts from the day course description and the syllabus is handed over to you. Part 2: Revising for tests and exams, shares revision techniques and a system that you can use to organize your studies. The procedure can make the course content for the tests or exams reduced to a single sheet of paper, but at the same time, you can recollect all the key topics, sub-topics, fundamental principles, main concepts, important terminologies, and major factors. Part 3, taking the tests or exams, highlights techniques including psychological techniques to mentally prepare you to answer the questions in a systematic way in order not to panic or fear when taking the tests or exams. This test or exam preparation system is necessary for test takers because as soon as anxiety sets in, the chances of losing your thoughts and rushing to answer questions with poor outcomes are very high.

In the conclusion section, summaries highlighting some key points to help you to apply the test prep guide and how to study for exams are provided. In the appendices section, Appendix 1 demonstrates an example of a typical syllabus to give the roadmap to academic success; Appendix 2 covers mnemonics to provide tools for studying usually arranged topics to help reduce a whole book to an one-pager revision note. On the other hand, Appendix 3 provides the summary of learning and studying tips that can be employed.

PART 1

80-20 STRATEGY: PREPARING FOR TESTS AND EXAMS

2.0 PREPARING FOR TESTS AND EXAMS

2.1 Test Passing or Exam Passing System – The 80/20 Strategy

The test passing system or exam passing system is a mental tool developed to systematically boost students' confidence when learning or studying, revising and taking exams or tests. The 80/20 strategy assumes that all topics in the syllabus to be taught and examined on have different levels of understanding. Some are easy whereas others are difficult to understand.

Equipped with this key information, right from the beginning of the semester you must begin to make serious observations and begin to rank the topics accordingly. That is, rank 80% of the overall topics as easy to understand and 20% difficult to understand. The initial benefit is that during the semester, you can then make efforts to seek help immediately from the Professor, Teaching Assistants and sometimes colleagues to help your understanding of those 20% difficult to understand topics.

It may turn out that by the time of revision for an exam or test or a quiz or assignment, the degree of understanding of the topics might have changed. In this case, you have to re-rank the topics during the revision period. During the revision week, you should focus on mastering the easy to understand 80% topics and of course still make an effort to understand the 20% of more difficult topics.

With these preparations and revision rankings, during exams, by this 80/20 strategy for passing tests and exams, first you must focus on completing the first 80% of the number of questions you are to answer according to the ranked easy to understand 80% topics. When you finish answering the 80% of the questions, according to this system, you should be in the passing range if you answer questions correctly. When you finish with the 80% you must use the remaining time to respond to the remaining 20% difficult to understand topics and their related questions. If you are able to finish this last 20% of the questions, this then puts your grade above 80% and potential to get at least B and most likely an A.

This is the rationale behind this book. Hence, when this 80/20 strategy is practiced and applied to any test and exam, you are certain to always pass. This 80/20 strategy is applicable not only to standard tests and final exams, but also all tests including homework assignments, class assignments, projects, quizzes, and midterm exams.

2.2 Test and Exam Prep Activities at the Beginning of the Semester

2.2.1 First Day of the Course

Meeting the Professors and the Significance of the Syllabus

Preparing for tests and exams, and hence getting higher scores, excellent grades and higher GPAs begin from the very first day a class commences and when the teacher providsthe syllabus for the course. Typically, the professor will explain the curriculum which will typically include purpose or aims or goals and objectives of the course, course descriptions, learning outcomes, course outlines or topics and subtopics, and course requirements including course evaluation criteria and grading schemes. Usually, most students will ignore the components of the syllabus after the first day of class and only focus on day-to-day teaching without paying serious attention to the syllabus. For the purpose of this guide, an example of a typical syllabus is available in Appendix 1.

During your first meeting with the professor, before you leave the class, you need to make sure you understand each of the sections of the syllabus. The curriculum will set limits and serve as your roadmap for the remaining part of the program or semester. Failure to understand the role of the syllabus in your educational life for that semester and all other semesters, and especially the course evaluation criteria and merely treating it as routine information of no significance is the beginning of your academic problems and challenges. When this happens, you will likely struggle throughout the semester, find it difficult to understand and follow the teachings of the professor and test-taking anxieties will become a daily occurrence.

To avoid these anxieties, you MUST regularly review the syllabus for every class you attend and make sure you follow it throughout the semester. Unless in exceptional cases, most often the teacher does not deviate from the curriculum. The syllabus serves as a tripartite contract between the teacher, student, and the college/school. Vital!

Why You Must Focus on All Components of the Syllabus

With the curriculum made available to you, you MUST spend considerable time to understand and regularly follow the various sections. This will typically cover course goals, aims, objectives, descriptions, outcomes, requirements, evaluation, grading scheme, textbooks, and references.

From the course requirements, you should know the percentages of the course assessment criteria that constitute 100%. For different colleges, programs and countries, course evaluation criteria vary. However, a typical example of a course evaluation is as shown below:

- Attendance: 5%
- Quizzes: 5%
- Assignment/Homework: 10%
- Project: 10%
- Laboratory/Practical: 10%
- Industrial or field visit: 5%
- Internship: 5%
- Midterm exams: 20%
- Final examinations: 30%

Similarly, from the course requirements, you should recognize the course grading scheme for that particular course. Classification system varies from colleges, programs, and countries. However, a representative course grading system is as shown below:

- A: 90%-100%
- B: 80%-89%
- C: 70% -79%
- D: 60%- 69%
- F: less than 59%

It is now your duty to understand and follow the course criteria and grading scheme regularly throughout the semester. Following this is essential for achieving higher scores and grades. This is because, if for example the class rules for attendance is 5% and you fail to attend classes you will lose this score. What this means is that at the end of the semester your score will reduce to 95%.

Also, assuming, there is one laboratory work which is 10% according to the evaluation criteria given above. If you miss the lab work and do not turn in your report, at the end of the semester, the total score that will remain for you is 85%. Reviewing of the grading scheme indicates that you are already out of "A" grade which is 90% to 100%. Hence, if you are not able to score full marks on the remaining evaluation criteria, you will have to do extra work to get a "B." This way you have denied yourself an "A," and this will significantly affect your overall GPA.

On the other hand, if you attend classes, do all class and homework assignments, laboratory works/experiments, industrial visits, project, and internship, you will easily get a total of 50%. If you follow the exams preparation and taking technique to be taught soon, and get say 15% out of 20% on the midterm exams, you will achieve 65%. In this case, the remaining score is 30% for the final examination. Similarly, if you follow the exam preparation and taking technique in this guide, your minimum score on the test is expected to be 25% out of 30%. Your total score for the semester for that hypothetical course example will be 90% which is grade "A." This result will mean you will achieve and maintain a higher grade for that class and in this case GPA of 4.0.

As you can see from this illustrative example, using the combination of the evaluation criteria and grading scheme, a student cannot take any of the course assessment standards in the syllabus for granted. Right from the beginning of the semester, you must take every course evaluation criteria serious, and failure to do so will spell disaster for you at the end of the semester. Some students usually think they can play throughout the semester and take the final examination, but the final exam is only 30% in this case.

2.2.2 During the Semester

Understanding the Organization of the Course Description and the Course Outline

Course descriptions are characterized by definitions, the particular subject, topics, sub-topics, fundamental principles, main concepts and key terminologies. The way to understand each course is to make serious effort to understand the course description in addition to the course goals, objectives, and outcomes. The topics, subtopics, fundamental principles, main concepts and key terminologies of the course description form the foundation throughout the teachings of the course. Typically, course descriptions shall have an association with the course outlines or topics.

To understand the significance of course description, you need to conceive that every course is similar to learning a new language, and hence it comprises new terminologies. Some professors may list all the key terms and others may not. If the keywords are not in the syllabus, or you are not directed or instructed to look for the definitions of the key terminologies, you have to construct your own list from the course description and outline/topics, and define all the standard languages or key terminologies yourself. Make sure you understand the words from the beginning of the semester through to the end of the semester. Your understanding of the norm will improve your fluency of that course and make it easier to follow the class during teaching.

More importantly, the course description will give you a structure or organization of that course. An analogy of the structure or organization is a human being with head, body, and legs. An alternative analogy of structure and organization of a course description is a tree comprising leaves, trunk, and roots. From the structure and the organization of the course, you can understand how the course will unfold throughout the semester. Most likely, in the syllabus, the professor will break down the course description into a course outline which will be small sections comprising of topics and subtopics to cover throughout the syllabus. Understanding the course structure or its organization and its relationship with the course outline makes it easier to understand and follow the teachings.

When the syllabus does not show the course outline, you must make efforts to understand the organization or structure of the course description. You do this by deconstructing the course description into course outline yourself to guide you. Below is an example of course description for Introduction to Nanotechnology course I designed and taught at a university in the USA. In this course, as shown in appendix 1, I provided a course outline.

> "Nanotechnology with a concentration on broad areas of nanostructured materials; nanoscale devices; nanomanufacturing processes/techniques and systems; and machinery/equipment for nanoproduction and quality control; nano production systems; nano-business; and their interdisciplinary applications in various mechanical engineering technology such as material science, manufacturing processes, machine design, tool design and instrumentation and control".

Assuming there is no course outline, in this case, you have to decompose the course description into course outline yourself. To deconstruct a course description into course outline to help you follow the course throughout the syllabus requires an understanding of the course aims or goals, objectives and outcomes. After reviewing them, you can now analyze the course description and break it down. For example, the break down could look similar to the illustration below:

- Nanostructured materials - applications and relationship to material science
- Nanoscale devices - applications and relationship to machine design
- NanoManufacturing processes/techniques and systems - applications and relationship with manufacturing systems
- Machinery/equipment for production and quality control - applications and connection to tool design and instrumentation and control
- Nano production systems
- NanoBusiness

As you can see, I am making an attempt to help me to understand the course organization to have a mental picture as to the constituents of the course. I, therefore, analyzed the course description and used my previous knowledge to form a structure that gave me a clear mental picture of what the course is all about. In the absence of a course outline, you will struggle to understand the course if you do not put in much effort to understand the course structure. This is because you will be forced to learn individual details and this could be many parts or read a whole book many times without having a simple structure to follow or guide you.

Also, you may choose to draw an organizational structure or flowchart to show how the deconstructed course description flows as a subject. You may not get the understanding 100% right from the beginning, but the efforts you put into analyzing the course description at the beginning and refining or improving it throughout the semester will give you a better appreciation of your expectation throughout the course. The benefits are that, as you gain a better understanding you will continue to deconstruct the course description which will eventually serve as a summary for your revision. As a result, the effort you put in at the beginning and throughout the semester will pay off at that end.

Preparing to Score High on Quizzes, Assignments, and Laboratories:

For the given course evaluation example, to assure yourself with grade "A" or at least a "B" grade at the end of a course, you need to guarantee and score maximum percentage scores on attendance, quizzes, assignments, projects, and laboratory or experiments. In preparing to attend a class, you need to keep the 80/20 strategy in mind, this will help you to focus and ask questions on the 20% difficult topics. Similarly, for quizzes, you must use the 80/20 strategy to revise for the quizzes. You must as well use the 80/20 strategy to take the quizzes.

Equally, for homework and class assignments, you must use the 80/20 to revise the topics and use the same strategy to prioritize your answers. That is you answer the 80% easier assignment questions first and later you do the 20% difficult questions. Likewise, you apply the 80/20 strategy to projects and laboratory works. Typically, the list of requirements you have to satisfy and hence you can apply the 80/20 strategy to guide you.

You will normally have control over these evaluation criteria except midterm and final tests and examinations. Scoring maximum percentages on all these evaluation criteria must be a top priority and you must start right from the beginning of the program and no other time.

Importance of Attendance

How do you achieve maximum scores on all the evaluation criteria? You cannot choose to absent yourself from classes. First, missing classes will make you lose scores. Secondly, it will make it difficult for you to understand the followon lessons. Thirdly, it will have collateral damages in terms of taking away your time from other subjects. Finally, the net effect of missing classes is that it will make it harder for you to answer questions.

To gain the maximum from attendance to enhance achieving higher scores on the evaluation criteria, while in class, you MUST make it a point to ensure you do not leave any class with doubts on your mind about the lesson. Some student feels shy to ask questions; they will be losers at the end. Remember, it takes the Professor several hours, days and weeks to prepare and teach a one-credit hour course. Therefore, if you miss a class, it will not be easy to make up for a three-credit hour class. It will take you days if not weeks and months to understand. Thus, the benefits of attending classes give you marks, but more importantly, it makes it easier for you to understand and follow the lessons and do well on all other assignments and tests applying the 80/20 strategy.

Quizzes

If you are in control of the syllabus as suggested, that is, regularly reviewing the syllabus to help you understand the course, attending classes and asking questions, reviewing your notes using the 80/20 strategy and practicing examples given by the professor, you should always score on your quizzes.

The key for scoring high on the quizzes is to make sure you do not leave your class without understanding lessons. You also have to practice! Practice! Practice! More examples and complete assignments on your own.

You have to apply the 80/20 strategy to review your notes for the quiz. Before quizzes are taken if you do not understand anything about the topic, especially, the 20% difficult topics, you must ask the professor or the teaching assistant for help.

Class and Homework Assignments

Similarly, if you are in control of the syllabus as suggested, that is, regularly reviewing the curriculum to understand, attending classes and asking questions, reviewing your notes according to the 80/20 rule and practicing examples given by the professor, you should always score high on your class assignments and home works.

The key to scoring high on the class and homework assignments is to make sure you do not leave your class without understanding the lessons. With the help of the 80/20 rule, you should be able to know the 20% difficult topics, and hence, if you have questions, ask the professor before you leave the class. Additionally, when professors give assignments, you must first study the instructions and problems. And if you do not understand clearly, you must immediately consult your Professor or the Teaching Assistant for advice before the due date for the assignment.

Further, you can also join a group to discuss the homework assignments, and after that, each will have to answer his/her questions applying the 80/20 strategy and submit before or on the due date. There is no reason why you should lose 1% or 2% by missing assignment due date.

Laboratory Experiments and Projects

For laboratory tests and project works, make sure you follow the instructions and rubrics. Complete the laboratory tests and projects according to the instructions. If you have questions during laboratory and project works, make sure you ask the professor or teaching assistant for guidance.

Complete the laboratory/project reports according to the instructions and submit before or on the due date. Following the instructions and rubrics and asking questions when in doubt will facilitate the achievement of the desired score and grades. Also apply the 80/20 strategy to help you complete projects and lab works. That is, based on the instructions given for either the project or lab works, you must determine how you will correctly apply the 80/20 rule and apply so that you can finish comfortably without being under stress.

General Preparations for Any Test or Examination

The subsequent sections will focus on techniques for passing any test or examination you may take. In general, for any test or exams, the following steps must be religiously followed:

1. Review the syllabus and make notes on the major topics or course outline for the course using the 80-20 strategy as a guide.
2. Look for at least past five years examination questions on that course and particularly from the professor who teaches the course, review the previous questions and make notes on the format of the test questions. You can also use the past questions for practice. Always utilize the 80/20 rule to help with revisions and for answering the practice questions.
3. Note the instructions, time allocated, variations in the issues and more importantly the number of questions and match the

number of questions with the topics and subtopics in the course outline or course description.

4. Usually, the syllabus should state the number of questions and the form of questions for the test, but not the specific questions. If these are not available in the syllabus, you should ask the Professor for guidance.

5. For midterm exams, review course outline or topics and subtopics up to the midterm, but for the final examination, appraise all themes and subtopics covered from the beginning of the semester to the time for the final exam. Employ the 80/20 strategy to review and to answer the questions.

6. During the revision period, you now have to prioritize and summarize all the major topics and subtopics based on several factors including tips and hints that were given by the professor and rank the issues/topics from easiness to difficulty of understanding using the 80/20 strategy. Use abbreviations and mnemonics to help summarize your notes.

7. In taking the test or exam answer easiest questions first by employing the 80/20 strategy.

PART 2

80-20 STRATEGY: REVISING FOR THE EXAMS AND TESTS

3.0 REVISION PRACTICES BEFORE TAKING EXAMS AND TESTS

Recall
Context
Scan
Read
Groups
Participate
Skim
Index
Library
Textbooks
Mnemonics
Retain
Mnemonics
Preread
Visual
Graph
STUDY
Review
Internet
Strategies
Graph
SKILLS
Memorization
Flowchart
Draw
Flashcards
Time Management
Success
Write
Notetaking
Concentrate
Outline
Listening
Draw
Learning Styles
Organize
Notebooks
Scan
Learning
Summarize
Index

3.1 At the Beginning of the Revision Period

Revisions do not apply to only midterm or final exams, but they also apply to revising for quizzes, assignments, projects, and laboratory experiments in order to give precise and brief answers. However, particularly, terminal exams, you are going to take tests or exams for your future and to advance your career.

For all revisions, you need to focus and discipline yourself that you have an important task, and that you have been preparing for several months. As a result, you need to be far-reaching and focused during the revision period. Do not allow distractions, because the review shall increase your chances of passing on all tests and getting better grades.

For the midterm or final exams or any test, the syllabus should provide information about the topics, the form of questions and when to take the examination. If these are not available in the syllabus, during the revision period the professor may emphasize the topics to be covered, the number and type (multiple choice or essay or combination of essay and multiple) of questions to answer in the exams.

If the professor does not state the topics, areas and number questions, you must ask the teacher in the class. You do not lose anything for seeking clarification from the Professor on the topical areas for the exams when not available in the syllabus. YOU CAN NOT ASK ABOUT THE PARTICULAR QUESTIONS, BUT YOU CAN ASK ABOUT THE TOPICS FROM WHICH THE QUESTIONS WILL BE SET. This helps you to narrow down on the themes to review before taking the exams.

3.2 Plan the Revision

Determine the topics and subtopics to cover for the exams either from the syllabus or the Professor, and use the 80/20 rule to prioritize the topics and/or subtopics. The number of themes and subtopics, either from the curriculum or the teacher will indicate the nature of questions for the exams; however, you will never know the specific questions.

Now being armed with topical areas and nature of questions for the exams, and whether essay or objective questions, begin to plan from the topics. Using the 80/20 rule, predetermine which themes and sub-topics that were easier for you to understand during your studies. If the number of easier topics is more than the harder ones, then you are on your way to success.

If the number of difficult topics is more than the easier ones, then you did not understand the course during the semester, and there will be challenges to overcome before you can pass. In this case, with the help of the 80/20 rule you will need to double your efforts to understand the topics so you can answer questions correctly and pass the exams.

3.3 Revision structure

With the aid of the 80/20 strategy, organize your review and rank the topics according to the easiest, followed by the simpler and most complicated issues for you to understand. This ranking will need to be predetermined to become the order by which you intend to answer questions during the exams according to the 80/20 rule.

If your easiest topics are less than the complicated ones, you need to make an effort to understand some of the difficult topics to make up in order to meet the conditions for the 80/20 rule. Otherwise, taking the exams to pass successfully will be a challenge.

3.4 Actual Revision Efforts

There could be several stages of revisions, however, use at least three steps to summarize each topic into a notebook during the review period. The minimum three stages during the study period are as follows:

- **First Revision:** Review the entire lecture notes or presentation of a particular course and summarize the course into at most ten (10) pages. Applying the 80/20 strategy, write down the major topics, subtopics, and key points with supporting facts. Start introducing abbreviations and mnemonics during the summary. Use the knowledge gained to *practice, practice, and practice* different examples on the same topic. The practice will help you to understand the topics from which questions are likely to be drawn.

• **Second Revision:** Further with the aid of the 80/20 rule, review the ten (10) page notes with supporting elaborations and summarize the notes further to at most five (5) pages. During the study, if some points are not clear, you can refer to the main notes or presentation or the 10 page summarized notes. Introduce more abbreviations and mnemonics at this stage. Again, use the knowledge acquired to practice, practice, and practice different examples. Again the practice will help to make sure you have complete understanding and control of the topics which will form the basis for the exam questions. Additionally, the practice will help make you become familiar with the mnemonic devices you developed.

• **Third Revision:** Again with the assistance of the 80/20 rule, review the five (5) pages summarized notes and re-summarize into at most one (1) page. At this stage, you need to use a lot of techniques including more abbreviations and mnemonics that will enable you to mimic or summarize a whole subject or topic or subtopics or factors. Repeatedly, practice recollecting information from memory using the abbreviations and mnemonics several times before the exams date. Appendix 2 provides a reference about how mnemonics techniques are applied to shorten a whole topic of one or more pages into a simple word.

Repeat using the abbreviations and mnemonics to recollect a whole course into one page. Additionally, practice, practice and practice by applying your understanding of the topics to answer more examples. These repetitions will ensure that abbreviations and mnemonics become more familiar. More importantly, the repeated practices of answering a variety of sample questions give you confidence and control before you take the exams or tests. More than likely the professor or the course will provide examples, or you can get more examples from the class assignments, homework assignments, and past exams.

3.4 The Morning before Taking the Exams

You need to allocate enough time similar to the time to write the exams. With the aid of the 80/20 strategy, use the time allocated to recollect from memory all the topics which you plan to answer questions on.

Hence, the morning before the exams while in bed or at a calm location, you need to review the 1-page summary by mentally recalling all the topics, sub-topics, fundamental principles, main concepts, and key factors in the notes which shall form the basis for possible questions to answer in the exam. If you can do this with a deep understanding without rushing, your chances of understanding the questions and answering them correctly during the exam or test are extremely high.

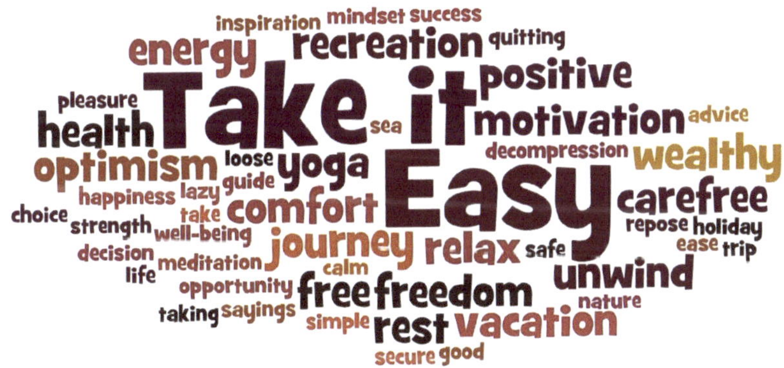

PART 3

TAKING THE EXAMS AND TESTS

4.0 80-20 STRATEGY: TAKING THE EXAMS AND TESTS

4.1 In the Examination Room

4.1.1 80/20 Psychological Preparation

To prevent anxiety, you need to relax but be alert in the exam room knowing that you have already prepared very well using the prescribed approach to prepare for the midterm or final exams. To further reduce anxieties, psychologically, you have to plan your answers in two stages, first plan to solve at least 80% of the questions and save time to answer the remaining 20% at the closing end of the allocated exam time.

That is, assuming you are to answer 5 out of 8 essay questions, 80% will consist of 4 questions. Similarly, assuming you are to answer 60 multi-choice questions, 80% will consist of 48 multi-choice questions. By this technique, considering the essay type questions, first, you answer the 4 questions. Psychologically, by answering these 4 questions that you have studied and practiced their topics very well, you will never fail and will certainly pass upon completion.

However, the whole purpose of following this test preparation and exam taking technique is to aim at scoring an "A" on all courses so that when the worse happens, you can make at least a "B." Therefore after completing the 4 questions, you would have to save time to answer the last one question, and that will put you in the "A" range. How to plan and allocate time to achieve this will be demonstrated in the subsequent sections. Further assumptions underlining this psychological approach is that you would have followed part 1 and 2 of this guide, and hence you know exactly the easiest topics to answer for your five (5) out of the eight (8) questions.

4.1.2 Category and Type of Questions to Anticipate

4.1.2.1 Types of Multiple-Choice Questions to Expect

Detailed information is not provided on multiple-choice questions because you are familiar with multiple-choice questions which come in different formats. Either from the syllabus and by reviewing past questions from a particular professor or the professor providing guidance, you will know the arrangement of the multiple choice questions to expect. In general, however, types of multiple-choice questions include the following formats:

- Fill in the blanks or sentence completion
- Select one answer from two or more answers
- True or false

The purpose of knowing the various types of multiple-choice questions before taking the exams is to assist you in developing the strategy for solving the different types of multiple-choice questions that will show up in the actual exams. Being armed with such information will reduce anxiety when in the examination room to take the test. More importantly, as described in the earlier, you still need to apply the psychological technique on yourself to eliminate anxieties by knowing ahead of time which types of multiple-choice questions are easier and harder and rank them before the exams.

4.1.2.2 Types of Essay Questions to Expect

Similarly, essay type questions come in different formats. Either from the syllabus or by reviewing past questions from a particular professor you will know the format of the issues to expect. In general, the type of essay questions to expect and learn how to answer include the following basic forms:

- **Define:** State exactly the key terms.

- **Describe:** Define, identify an overall structure or system, subsystem, components and parts. (As an aid to understanding and learn how to answer a description question, picture a structure similar to a human being as a system with a head, body, and legs as subsystems. And head has skull, eyes, face and ears as components. Also, the body has hands, chest, and stomach as components. On the contrary, the leg has thighs, legs, and foot also as components).

- **Explain:** Define, identify key factors, elaborate or clarify the key factors by giving examples.

- **Discuss:** Argue, identify underlining theory, identify key factors to explain, identify limitations, merits, and demerits, advantages, and disadvantages

- **Compare A and B:** identify key criteria or factors, establish association between A and B, give at least one example of each to show comparison

- **Contrast A and B:** Differences or Distinction: Identify key criteria or factors, establish differences between A and B, give at least one example of each to show the difference

- **What are the similarities between A and B?** Identify key criteria or factors, establish association between A and B, give at least one example of each to show similarities

- **What are the differences between A and B?** Identify key criteria or factors, establish differences between A and B, give at least one example each to show the difference

- **List the factors:**

- **Give examples:**

- **List advantages and disadvantages**:

The purpose of knowing the various types of essay questions earlier so that you can develop an effective strategy for answering these kinds of questions. This way, you will not be stressing yourself in the examination room trying to understand a problem and losing time in the process. Well-armed with the prior knowledge of how to answer various types of questions, for example, as soon as you see a discussion or description question you will know how to answer them using the supporting facts you have acquired during the revision phase. Similarly, you will need to apply the psychological technique on yourself to eliminate anxieties by knowing ahead of time which of the essay type questions are easier and harder for you and rank them before the exams.

4.2 How to Prepare in Advance to Answer Likely Types of Questions

4.2.1 Steps for Answering Essay Type Questions

1. **Instructions:** When you receive the questions, first read the instructions very carefully and note the total time. Assume the total number of items is 8 and you are to answer 5, and time is 60mins. Usually, questions will be allocated similar marks, but

sometimes the questions will have different scores. For purposes of illustration let us assume each question carry the same mark.

2. **Plan Your Time:** Out of the total time 60 mins, use 5-10 mins to carefully read through all the essay questions and identify the topics you have previously studied and planned to answer questions. Do not panic! If you do not understand the problems, you cannot answer them, it is, therefore, important to use this small time to read through the questions before attempting to answer them.

3. **Rank Questions**: While reading through the questions after identifying the problems with the topics you are most familiar with and easy to understand, you need to re-prioritize or rank the questions according to easiness to answer. Also, while reading through the questions if an important point you have practiced occurs to you quickly note it down along that question.

4. **Allocate Equal Time to Each Question:** Now assuming all the questions have equal marks, divide the remaining 50 or 55mins into 5 that means, you will allocate at least 10mins to each question.

5. **Answer 80% of the Questions**: Using the psychological trick on yourself, initially, prepare to answer 80% of the questions out of the five required questions to answer. That means, for 4 out of 5 required questions, initially, make plans to answer four (4) questions carefully but within the planned time of 10mins to each question. You need to watch your time, if you use 10mins per answer, you have to move to the next question.

When you finish answering the four questions correctly without rushing, you are confident of passing the exams, and psychologically it reduces test-taking anxiety. This because you have responded to the questions accurately and had the facts to support the solutions.

You may gain or lose time on each question. If you're wasting time, it may come from the 10mins allocated to the last 20% difficult questions, and that should not be of major concern if you have answered the four questions correctly. It is better you answer at least 80% of the questions very well and score 80% rather than rushing through all the five questions and not doing well on any of them because of lack of strategy.

6. **Answer the Remaining 20% Difficult Questions:** If you gain time, it will be less stressful to answer the remaining 20% of the questions, for 5 required questions, that will be the fifth and last difficult question. Knowing, you have extra time on hand, you can use 10mins to answer the last 20% difficult questions, and psychologically it is a bonus for you to help you get an A. Thus, following the procedure up to this step 6, after answering the last 20% questions, in this example the fifth (5th) question, your chances of scoring above 80% and putting yourself in the 90% score range and hence getting an "A" is very high.

7. **Review the Answers:** If you save time, do not leave the examination room immediately. Complete any gaps left in your responses to the questions and correct errors or mistakes. Also, check your name, date, and back of the paper if it is paper exams, whether there are missing questions until the examination time is up and you hand over the paper.

Unfortunately, some students bluff and leave the exam room to show off that they have finished. That is a mistake. Taking examination is about your future, and it is important you do not look on your shoulders but rather focus like a laser to do very well.

4.2.2 Steps for Answering Multiple Choice Questions.

1. **Review Instructions:** Similarly, when you receive the questions, first read the instructions very carefully and note the total time. Assuming the number of items is 60 and time is 60mins. This means one minute per question. Hence, the strategy is different; you cannot read through all the questions before answering them. Conscious of your expected topics, you respond to the questions as you read each question, but apply the 80:20 psychological trick to the multiple choice questions to avoid anxieties. That means you plan to answer 80% of the questions first with confidence based on the easiest topics and when you save time to complete your last 20% of the questions from the difficult topics.

80%

2. **Strategy for Prioritizing Answers to 80% of the Questions:** Applying the 80:20 rule, you respond to the 80% of questions according to easiness, answering the questions logically as you read through the question paper. As you answer the questions systematically, mark or leave out the 20% of the difficult questions containing topics that you are not familiar with or difficult for you to understand. Failure to do this, as you can see, in this example, it is one minute per question, and hence you will lose time, and you cannot finish when you spend too much time on one question.

3. **Answering Technique:** Use elimination to select the correct answers. That means, after reading the question, review the answers, and rule out the unlikely answers to narrow down your answers to at most 2 and select the right one.

4. **Review and Answer Last 20% of the Questions:** After answering last of the 80% difficult questions, you may have saved time. You then have to return and restart from the beginning and answer the questions you marked as challenging and time-consuming..

5.0 CONCLUSION

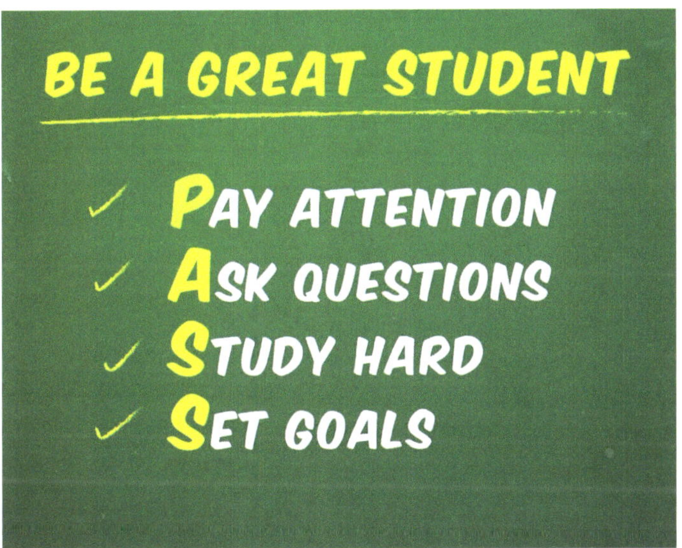

5.1 The Testing Preparation System

To successfully prepare and get excellent scores and complete your program with good grades, you should understand and follow the system religiously from the beginning of the semester. The major components of the test preparation and taking system that should guide you are:

5.1.1 **Follow the syllabus from the beginning of the program**

5.1.2 **Follow test revision strategies**

5.1.3 **Follow exam taking strategies**

5.2 Getting Higher Scores:

Getting good grades at the end of a program requires scoring above 90% on all test evaluation criteria or meeting all course requirements including

5.2.1 **Attendance:** 100% attendance

5.2.2 **Assignments**: Completing and submitting all class and homework assignments with the aid of the Professor or teaching assistant or group study if necessary before or on the due date

5.2.3 **Experiments and Projects:** Seek advice from the teacher or teaching assistant if needed, and complete and submit all experiments and project reports before or on the due date.

5.2.4 **Midterm and Final exams:** Use the syllabus to guide you, know and understand the topics and sub-topics from which questions will be set. During the semester study and practice! Practice! Practice! many examples to demonstrate and confirm your understanding, revise before the examination day, and answer questions according to the 80:20 psychological strategy to reduce test-taking anxiety in order not to rush and make more mistakes. The 80:20 psychology trick when followed in the exam, your chances of getting at least a "B" is always guaranteed. Additional effort will always put you in the "A" range. This is how to get "A"s and "B"s.

5.3 Study Tips

You should always learn or review as if you are organizing items into a drawer or papers into a folder sequentially and logically. Learning throughout the semester should be interesting and easier. Therefore, whenever you are studying, and it appears to be difficult, it means you are doing something wrong. Most likely you did not prepare very well from the beginning of the semester, you missed classes, you did not understand the terminologies, and you did not pay attention to follow the syllabus to give you the mental picture of the overall course and/or to use the curriculum as the roadmap from the beginning of the semester.

5.4 Mnemonics as Study and Revision Aid

Design and use your own mnemonics devices during your study and practice often during any revision period to help you reduce your notes to 1 page. The mnemonic devices will help you for easy recollection during examinations, quizzes, and tests. Apply mnemonics to learn most of the topics that require for example the following:

5.4.1 Give examples

5.4.2 List factors

5.4.3 Use factors to compare or contrast or describe or explain two or more subjects or topics

5.4.4 Use criteria to compare or contrast or describe or explain two or more subjects or topics

5.4.5 Logically produce a list say the arrangement of the planet or elements on the periodic table.

5.5 Happy moment

If you follow this test preparation guide and apply 80:20 test or exam taking method from the beginning of the semester through to the end of the semester, please go home at the end of the semester, sleep peacefully and expect favorable final results for each course with pleasing "A" and "B" grades and excellent GPA. You will be smiling!

REFERENCES

1. Mnemonic - Example Problems. (n.d.). Retrieved from www.exampleproblems.com/wiki/index.php/Mnemonic

2. Mnemonic (n.d.). Retrieved from www.spiritus-temporis.com/mnemonic/examples-of-simple-mnemonics.html

3. Juta - Exam and study skills. (n.d.). Retrieved from http://juta.co.za/academic/pages/academic-survival-101

4. Mnemonics (n.d) www.real-memory-improvement.com/examples-of-mnemonics.html

APPENDICES

Appendix 1

SAMPLE SYLLABUS: INTRODUCTION TO NANOTECHNOLOGY

Dr. David Addie Noye, Adjunct Professor

COURSE SYLLABUS

Catalog Description

Nanotechnology with a concentration on broad areas of nanostructured materials; nanoscale devices; nanomanufacturing processes/techniques and systems; and machinery/equipment for nanoproduction and quality control; nanoproduction systems; nanobusiness; and their interdisciplinary applications in various mechanical engineering technology such as material science, manufacturing processes, machine design, tool design and instrumentation and control.

Course Goals

Nanotechnology promises immense benefits to society. The benefits include reduced manufacturing costs, reduced dependence on fossil fuels, reduced environmental pollution, improve medical technologies among others. This course is an introductory nanotechnology course, aimed at preparing students for further industrial or academic work in the field of preparing technical specifications; designing; fabrication and characterization of advanced nanostructured materials, nanoscale devices, and machinery/equipment for nanoscale production, and nanoproduction systems.

Additionally, it helps students identify and subsequently advance their future interests in researching in new generation advanced nanostructured materials or nanoscale device fabrication techniques. Furthermore, it will prepare students for technical positions in advanced manufacturing, quality control, sales and marketing of nanotechnology materials, devices, production machinery, metrology equipment, and instruments. Students will also be able to participate in consulting engineering works related to the design of manufacturing systems for the production of nanotechnology products.

Course Objectives

The course content has been structured to help the student achieve the following objectives:

To identify and develop a career path in the multidisciplinary field of nanotechnology.

To gain an understanding of the principles of nanotechnology; characterization of nanostructured materials; imaging and manipulation techniques; design of nanomanufacturing processes and production machinery; and design of tools and equipment for fabricating and assembling and measuring at the nanoscale.

To acquire additional skills in the design of clean rooms for nanomanufacturing systems and entrepreneurial know-how on the strategic importance of establishing nanobusiness.

To generate interest in the research, design and development of nanotechnology for future advancement.

Required Texts

Ratner, D. & Ratner, M. (2003). Nanotechnology: A gentle introduction to the next big idea. New Jersey: Pearson Education Inc.

Kannangara, K; Raguse, B., Simmons, M., Smith, G., & Wilson, N. (2002). Nanotechnology: Basic science and emerging technologies. New York: Chapman & Hall/CRC. ISBN: 1-58488-339-1.

Reference Materials

Bainbridge, W. S. & Roco, M. C. (Eds.) (2002). Societal Implications of Nanoscience and Nanotechnology. Kluwer Academic Publishers

Nicolini, C. (1996). Molecular manufacturing. New York: Plenum Press.

Drexler, K. E. (19920). Nanosystems: Molecular Machinery, Manufacturing, and Computation. New York: John Wiley & Sons, Inc.

Cammarata, R. C. & Edelstein, A. S. (1998). Nanomaterials: synthesis, properties, and applications.

Lyshevski, S. E. (2000). Nano-and Macro-Electromechanical systems: fundamentals of nano and micro engineering (Vol. 1). ISBN: 0849309166.

Lyshevski, S. E. (2002). MEMS and MEMS: systems, devices, and structures (Vol. 2). ISBN: 0849309166.

COMSOL Multiphysics modeling and simulation software by COMSOL. www.COMSOL.com

Internet Sources

ASME Nanotechnology Institute. www.nanotechnologyinstitute.org

EUSPEN (European Union Precision Engineering and Nanotechnology). www.euspen.org

Foresight Institute. www.foresight.org

Information on Nanotechnology. www.nanomagazine.com

Institute of Nanotechnology. www.nano.org.uk

National Nanotechnology Initiative. www.nano.gov

Scientific American Nanotech Directory. www.sciam.com/nanotech_directory.cfm

Course Outline

Nanotechnology-Introduction

Introduces Nanotechnology and deals with background and fundamental science behind nanotechnology. Definition of nanotechnology; Historical background; Concept of nanotechnology fabrication; Nanoscience-Fundamental science behind nanotechnology; and Nanotechnology challenges.

Nanotechnology-Nanostructured Materials

Involve nanoscale surface and interface processes and relationships between nanostructures and properties. Smart materials; Nanotubes-properties, applications and production; and Nanocomposites

Nanotechnology-Components Production and Assembling Techniques

Covers fundamental nanoscale processes. Introduction to molecular manufacturing; Molecular Synthesis; Nanoscale Assemblers, Self Assembly, Top-Down and Bottom-up Assembly; Nanolithography techniques - introduction to lithography, conventional lithography, electron beam lithography, deep pen lithography; Nanoscale or thin film deposition processes; Electrospinning; Molecular Beam Epitaxy (MBE); Chemical Vapor Deposition (CVD); and Electron Physical Vapor Deposition (EPVD) Processes; Langmuir-Blodgett Method (LB)

Nanotechnology-Production and Quality Control Equipment

The goal is to address specific machinery and equipment for physical production and measuring of nanoscale phenomena, materials, and devices. This will concentrate on tools to make and assemble and measure nanostructures and how to design this equipment. Specific equipment covered will include Scanning Electron Microscope (SEM), Scanning tunneling microscope (STM), High-Resolution Scanning tunneling microscope (HRSTM), Scanning probe microscopes (SPM); Atomic force microscope (AFM);

Nanoscale Devices and Their Applications

This will center on the impact of nanoscale phenomena on nanoscale device and systems performance/function, integration, and packaging. It will specifically include Industrial applications; Consumer goods; Optical applications; Nanosensors; Electronic applications; NEMS/MEMS; and Biological applications - drugs & drug delivery, photodynamic therapy, molecular motors, protein engineering, nanoluminscent tags.

NanoProduction Systems

The objective is to show the impact of nanoscale phenomena on the functions and performance of manufacturing systems for nanoscale production. This will encompass an introduction to clean technology; classification of clean rooms; design of clean-room systems.

NanoBusiness and NanoEthics

Nanotechnology-the next industrial revolution; the structure of contemporary nano business; forecasting the trend in nanotechnology business-high-tech, biotech, nanotech; and investment outlook for nanotechnology businesses. Starting your nanotechnology venture. In addition, ethical implications of nanotechnology on society and management of nanotechnology ethical dilemmas will be covered.

Grading Criteria

The final grade for the course will be based on the following allotments:

Activity Percentage

Attendance 10%
Class Participation 10%
Quizzes 20%
Exercises 20%
Laboratory demonstration/industrial visit reports 10%
Design Project 30%
Total 100%

Letter Grade Key

A: 90-100%
B: 80-89 %
C: 70-79 %
D: 60-69%
F: 0-59%

Course Requirements and Organization

Lectures

Lectures will be given to describe the fundamental principles and concepts of nanotechnology. This will require attendance by every student.

Class Attendance:

Attendance is required for all scheduled lectures and final presentation by students. There will be deduction of marks for students who absent themselves without prior permission.

Class Participation

This will require completion of weekly readings and active participation in class based on these readings. In addition, this will require participating in the final presentation to be made by graduate students.

Quizzes

Four (4) Quizzes will be given during the semester covering lectures and assigned readings. The quizzes will consist of multiple choice(s), and/or true or false answer formats. There will be no opportunity to make up missed quizzes.

Exercises

There shall be four (4) exercises, each scoring 5%. Exercise 1, will cover nanotechnology-introduction and nanostructured materials; exercises 2- nanocomponents production and assembling techniques, exercise 3- production and quality control equipment used in nanofabrication; and exercise 4, nanotechnology-applications and nanoscale devices, nanoproduction systems and nanobusiness & nanoethics.

Design Project

Students are required to submit a completed design project. It is expected to be a final design concept following the design process with preliminary design calculations of a tool, nanoscale manipulator, nanoscale device, nanoproduction equipment among others. The topic could be proposed by the student. The Professor may also supply diverse but relevant design topics to be chosen by students. The design topic and presentation should be relevant to the course content. The topic and a written design brief, describing the topic should be submitted three (3) weeks after commencement of class for approval. The design report, about 8-10 pages in a departmental format should be submitted on the day of the presentation. The format of the design report will be provided by the Professor to all students on the first day of the class. Additionally, all students are to be present during the presentation.

Laboratory Demonstration/Industrial Visit.

Students will be exposed to practical operations and experimental demonstrations of equipment used for nanofabrication and characterization. This will be supplemented with field visits to industrial sites and nanotechnology centers with nanotechnology fabrication equipment.

Disabilities Act

The Americans with Disabilities Act of 1990 (ADA) provides protection from discrimination for qualified individuals with disabilities. Students with a disability, who require assistance, will need to contact the office of Disability Services (ODS) for coordination of academic accommodations.

Appendix 2

Use of Mnemonics as Revision Aids

1.0 What is Mnemonics?

Mnemonics is employed as a memory aid. The theory underlining mnemonics is that the human mind easily remembers data which are connected to personal, spatial and other meaningful information than that occurring in sequences that are meaningless.

Typically, mnemonics are verbal and sometimes stated as a verse. Most often mnemonics are employed to remember lists. They depend on repetitions to remember facts and associations between easy-to-remember constructs and lists of data.

A common mnemonic device that is employed to remembering lists consists of an easily remembered word, phrase, or rhyme whose initials or other characteristics are associated with the list items. As an example, the mnemonic devices are often used to memorize hard-to-break passwords.

2.0 Examples of mnemonics

2.1 Astronomy

To orderly name the planets starting from the Sun, the following phrases are often used:

"My Very Easy Memory Jingle Seems Useful Naming Planets,"
"Mary's Violet Eyes Made John Stay Up Nights Proposing,"
"My Very, Educated Mother Just Showed Us Nine Planets"

2.2 Biology, Medicine & Anatomy

To remember the 12 cranial nerves "Olfactory, Optic, Occulomotor, Trochlear, Trigeminal, Abducent, Facial, Auditory, Glossopharyngeal, Vagus, Accessory, and Hypoglossal," a popular mnemonic device used and it is stated as follows:

"Oh Oh Oh, To Touch And Feel A Girl, Very Sexy And Hot."

2.3 Chemistry

To remember redox reactions chemistry students often use the mnemonic device. Two versions available are:

Use of the phrase "LEO says GER," LEO means Loss of Electrons is Oxidation, and GER mean Gain of Electrons is Reduction.

Use of the word "OIL-RIG." The OIL means Oxidation Is Loss, and RIG means Reduction Is Gain (of electrons).

2.4 Engineering

To remember which way to turn common right handed bolts, screws, nuts, and light bulbs engineers and technicians use the mnemonic device:

"Lefty loosey, righty tighty."

2.5 Mathematics

2.5.1 In mathematics, mnemonics devices have been used to remember the digits of pi. This is made up of phrases or verses in which successive digits of pi are derived by counting the number of letters in each word. Examples of the mnemonics used are:

"May I have a number?"(May = 3, I = 1, have = 4, etc. 3.1415)
"May I have a large container of coffee?" (3.1415926)

2.5.2 In high and secondary schools, students often remember the basic trigonometric functions with the phrase SOH-CAH-TOA

SOH: Sine = Opposite leg divided by the Hypotenuse
CAH: Cosine = Adjacent leg divided by the Hypotenuse
TOA: Tangent = Opposite leg divided by the Adjacent leg

2.6 Physics

In physics, the name Roy G. Biv is used to remember the order of the colors in the spectrum "Red, Orange, Yellow, Green, Blue, Indigo, Violet." The mnemonic used is stated as follows:

In England "Richard Of York Gave Battle In Vain" or

In England "Richard Of York Gave Birth In Vain" by replacing "Battle" with "Birth."

2.7 General Knowledge

In general and popular culture, the mnemonics used to remind
people that the best plan is often a simple plan which is "keep it
simple and stupid" is the word

K-I-S-S

Reference: www.spiritus-temporis.com/mnemonic/examples-of-simple-mnemonics.html

Appendix 3

Learning and Studying Tips for Preparing and Taking Examinations and Tests

Learning or studying is always similar to organizing a drawer or folder. And you start with the following:

1.0 Understand the catalog course description and the syllabus

2.0 Learn definitions of common terminologies that make up a course or subject correctly

3.0 Know how questions are set and how they are answered. Examples of key terms used in framing questions include:

- Define or Describe
- Compare or Similarities
- Contrast or Distinguish
- Explain or Discuss
- How?
- What?
- Which?
- When?

4.0 Review past questions to see the trend

5.0 Know what type of issues and level of difficulties you want to answer before you take any test or go into an examination room

6.0 Revise and summarize your notes and make use of mnemonics to help reduce a complete course or subject to 1 sheet of paper. Review at least three times before the due date of the exams, test or quiz.

7.0 Make sure you physically see the revised notes with eyes before you take the exams or tests.

8.0 On the day of the exams, set aside some hours equal to the examination time and try to review the 1 page summarized notes you prepared during the revision while in bed or on your way to make sure you can remember or recollect the mnemonics.

9.0 For psychological preparation, aim at answering 80% of the questions first, and if there is time, answer the remaining 20% of the questions to put you in score range above 80% and close to 100%.

ABOUT THE AUTHOR

Dr. David Addie Noye is a researcher, an engineering designer, an inventor, a professor and a serial entrepreneur. Dr. Noye is a USA citizen of Ghanaian descent. As past student and an Adjunct Professor, Dr. Noye understands educational system and hurdles students must go through to graduate successfully with good GPA. Being a serial entrepreneur, Dr. Noye has learned the up and downs in starting and growing businesses both internationally and in the United States. As a result, combining his academic, research, industrial and business experiences and skill sets, Dr. Noye is in the best and unique position to teach and share his experiences to help others.

Education Experience

Dr. Noye taught at Southern Polytechnic State University (Now part of Kennesaw University) in Marietta, Georgia as an Adjunct Professor where he introduced Nanotechnology to the University. Similarly, at the University of Northern Iowa, while pursuing his doctorate, as Graduate Assistant, Dr. Noye added and taught Nanotechnology at the University. At GRATIS Foundation as

Director of Engineering Design Center, Dr. Noye created various engineering design and manufacturing skills training courses for engineers and technicians in the industry. He also participated in preparing in engineering design standards for Ghana.

Business Experience

Dr. David Noye is the Founder/Chairman of NanoResearch Inc (www.nanoresearchinc.com), advanced research, design, development, invention, and commercialization firm. The company is located in Atlanta, Georgia at CollabTech of Georgia State University. He is also Co-founder and Chief Technology Officer of SmartEnergi Corp (www.smartenergicorp.com), a global energy product manufacturer, and distributor. In Georgia Aerospace in Atlanta, Georgia, Dr. Noye was the Director of Nanotechnology Research and pioneered the introduction of Nanotechnology into the Company.

Philanthropic Experience

Dr. Noye is also a philanthropist and Founded NanoLab Foundation to promote job and income generation infrastructure projects in the United States and overseas. To this end, Dr. Noye has spent several years of research and has developed proposals for creating Industrial Villages in the USA and abroad to accelerate job creation in the inner cities of the USA and developing economies of the world. In Ghana, Dr. Noye worked with GRATIS Foundation as Director of Engineering Design Center. Dr. Noye worked on numerous high profile projects funded by international organizations such as Canada International Development Agency and the European Union.

Professional Associations

Dr. Noye is a member of many professional organizations including Inventors Association of Georgia and American Society of Mechanical Engineers (ASME). Dr. Noye is also a member of Commerce Club in Atlanta, Georgia and can also be found on LinkedIn.

Academic Qualifications

Dr. Noye has doctorate in Industrial Technology with specialty in Nanotechnology from the University of Northern Iowa, Cedar Falls, Iowa in the USA, MSc in Engineering Design from Engineering Design Institute of Loughborough University, Loughborough, UK, Post-graduate Diploma in Production Management and Tool Design from India, and BSc in Mechanical Engineering from Kwame Nkrumah University of Science and Technology, Kumasi, Ghana.

CONNECT WITH DR. DAVID ADDIE NOYE

Connect to me LinkedIn: www.linkedin.com/in/drdanoye/
Friend me on Facebook: www.facebook.com/drdanoye
Follow me on Twitter: http://twitter.com/drdanoye
Favorite me at Smashwords:
www.smashwords.com/profile/view/drdanoye

###

Thank you for reading my book. If you enjoyed it, won't you please take a moment to leave me a review at your favorite retailer?

Thanks!

Dr. David Addie Noye